DAVE MATTHEWS BAND
BEFORE THESE CROWDED STREETS

Transcribed by Jeff Jacobson and Paul Pappas
Interior Photographs by Ellen Von Unwerth

Before These Crowded Streets is a crucial piece in the evolution of the

Dave Matthews Band, an album that retains the virtues of its multimillion-selling predecessors—1994's *Under the Table and Dreaming* and 1996's *Crash*—but takes them in bold new directions musically, lyrically, and instrumentally. The new album's 11 songs are given to chippy, dynamic arrangements, dramatic swells of sound, some of the most passionate vocals Matthews has ever performed, and passages of heartbreaking melancholy, boundless joy, and lust so pronounced that you might need a cold shower after listening to "Rapunzel" or "Crush." It is, in other words, a bold step forward for the band, but this kind of musical trailblazing is hardly unexpected.

Since emerging from Charlottesville, Virginia, in 1991, the Dave Matthews Band (Matthews, violinist Boyd Tinsley, saxophonist LeRoi Moore, bassist Stefan Lessard, and drummer Carter Beauford) has been lauded for its ambitious approach to music making. But the Dave Matthews Band's real palette, to this point, has been on the road, where its spirit of improvisation has made its concerts unique events, with no two ever alike.

Even though playing live remains a valued means of expression, Matthews said the band wanted to delve deeper into the studio recording process on *Before These Crowded Streets*. "We had a lot of songs we could have recorded,

songs that had developed on the road," Matthews says. But when he began conceiving the new album with producer Steve Lillywhite—who also produced *Crash*—both of them had a sense that "it would be nice to have new material."

Taking time off after the grueling *Crash* tour helped as well, according to Matthews. Though the group did hit the road for six weeks during the summer of 1997, a good chunk of the year was spent at home, playing and working on new ideas. "That was the first time I've been able to sit down in years," Matthews says. "I just listened to the air to see if I hadn't completely scared away the muse in me by screaming around the road. It was fun. It was a great inspiration to sit around . . . just playing and coming up with licks and ideas."

In the fall of 1997, the band repaired to the West Coast to begin recording with Lillywhite, putting bits of ideas together into songs. Not having a batch of tight, road-tested material worked to their benefit, says Matthews, who wrote the lyrics in New York City after the basic tracks had been recorded. "It was more exciting that we didn't know them," he explains. "We didn't know what to expect. They were constantly changing and constantly developing. The whole time we were thinking about it as an album, as a thing we had to finish rather than saying 'We have five out of ten songs done, we're halfway there.'" The result is a varied, thought-provoking soundscape with emotional shades of both dark and light. The first single, "Don't Drink the Water," is driven by a dark, foreboding groove and Matthews' menacing vocal. "Rapunzel" celebrates *amore*—"I worship women," Matthews explains. "The Last Stop" rides keening Middle Eastern scales and a stomping rhythm, while "Crush" echoes the classic sound of vintage Marvin Gaye. *Before These Crowded Streets* also houses some of Matthews' strongest lyrics yet, including some outwardly political messages in "The Last Stop" and "Don't Drink the Water," as well as darker sentiments in songs such as "Halloween," "Spoon," and "The Stone." "I think there's definitely a darker tone to a lot of these songs, maybe a little more burden to them," Matthews says. But, he notes, there's optimism as well; as he sings on "Pig," *"Just love will open our eyes/Just love will put the hope back in our minds."* "It still has the chemistry of the five of us playing together, which is a really positive experience for us. There's just a real joy of playing," he continues, "so I don't think the overall effect will be depressing."

As *Before These Crowded Streets* makes its way into the world, the Dave Matthews Band now plans to do what it always does—play live. The group is anxious to take its new material before audiences and watch it evolve in new directions. "I couldn't be happier, just musically, about how the five of us are turning out together," Matthews says. "Our ability to stay on track has shown itself. The music is still our focus, and I think that's evident."

DAVE MATTHEWS BAND   CARTER BEAUFORD   BOYD TINSLEY   STEFAN LESSARD   DAVE MATTHEWS   LEROI MOORE

CONTENTS

PANTALA NAGA PAMPA

Words and Music by
David J. Matthews

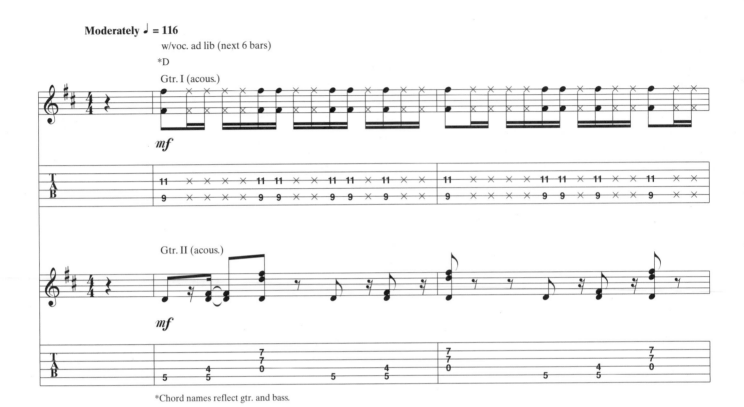

*Chord names reflect gtr. and bass.

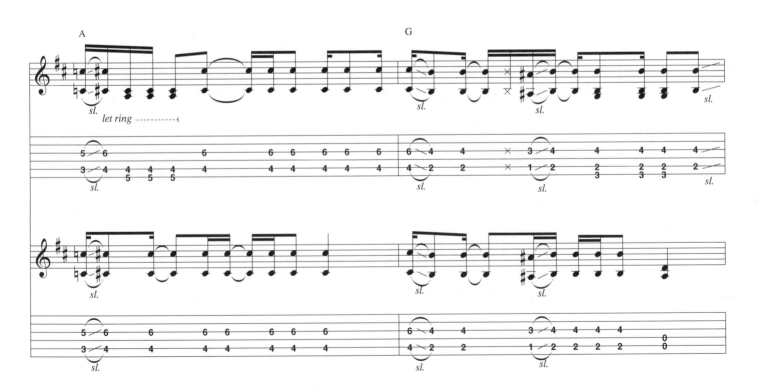

D

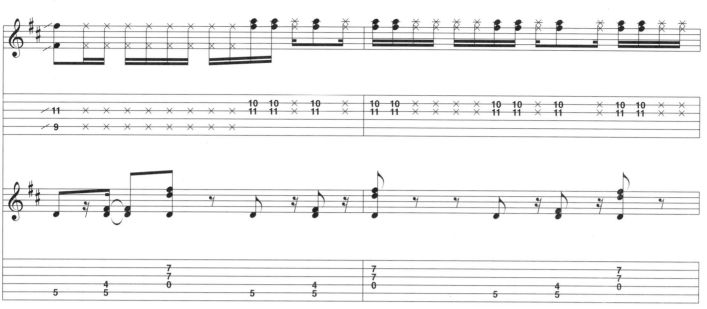

A6   G6

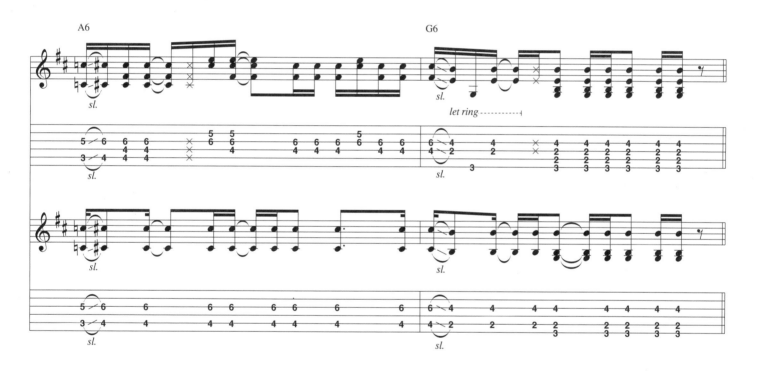

Em7   A7sus4

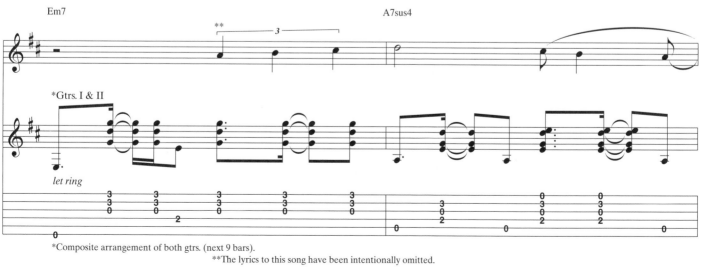

*Composite arrangement of both gtrs. (next 9 bars).

           **The lyrics to this song have been intentionally omitted.

*T = thumb

Segue to "Rapunzel"

8

RAPUNZEL

Words and Music by David J. Matthews,
Stefan Lessard, and Carter Beauford

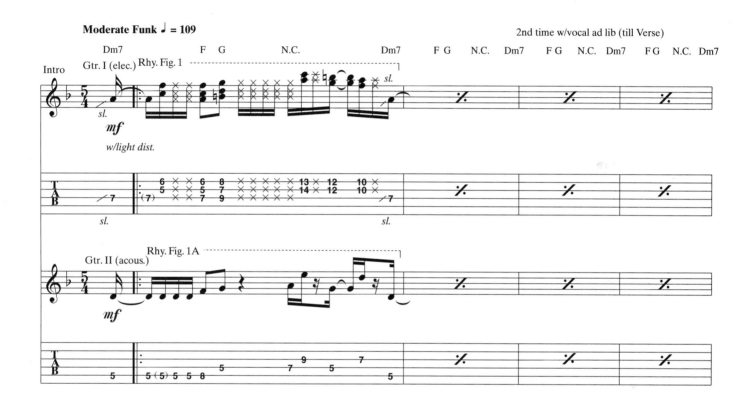

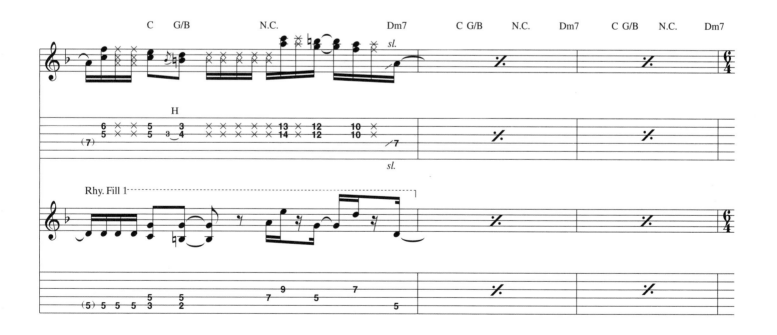

*Some chords implied by piano (throughout).

2nd time Gtr. I substitute Rhy. Fill 4

Rhy. Fill 4 (Gtr. I)

that I'll do my best for you, I do.
that I'll do my best for you, I do.

(end Rhy. Fig. 2)   Rhy. Fill 3

w/Rhy. Fig. 2
2nd time Gtr. I substitute Rhy. Fill 5

Love, let's stop to get it go - in'. Lost my - self just think -
Oh, for you I would crawl through the dark - est dun -

Gtr. I

Rhy. Fill 5 (Gtr. I)

*Substitute muted strings in parentheses when recalled.

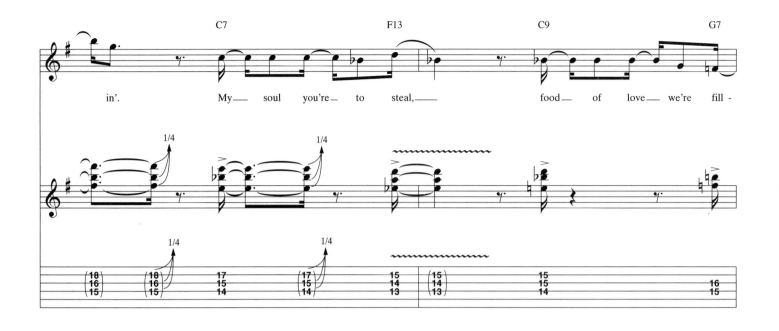

in'. My — soul you're — to steal, — food — of love — we're fill -

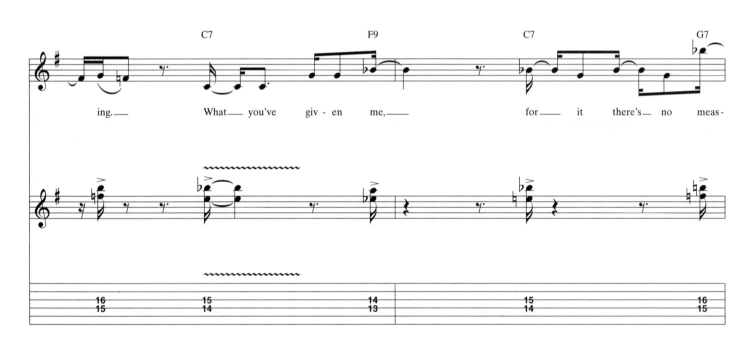

ing. — What — you've giv - en me, — for — it there's — no meas -

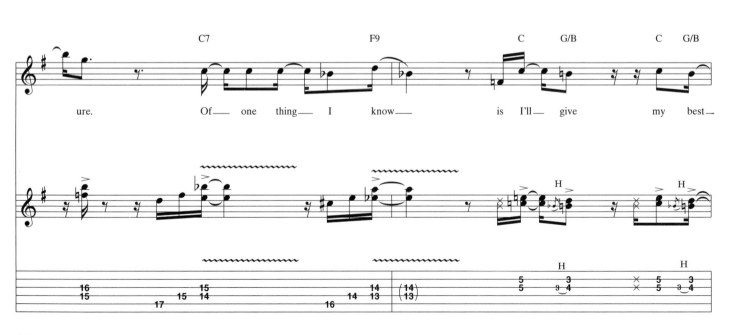

ure. Of — one thing — I know — is I'll — give my best —

16

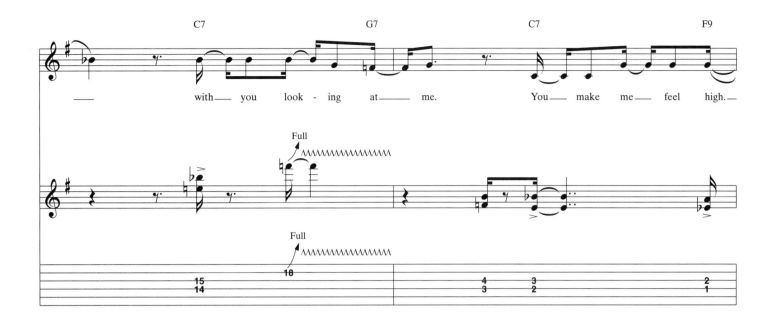

with— you look - ing at— me. You— make me— feel high.—

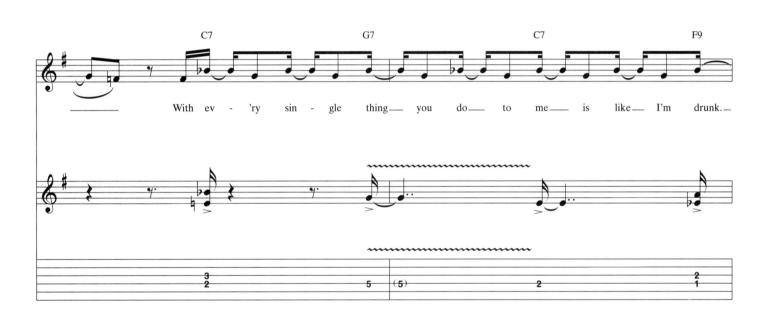

With ev - 'ry sin - gle thing— you do to me is like— I'm drunk.—

w/Rhy. Fill 3

I— do my best— for you, I do.—

Outro

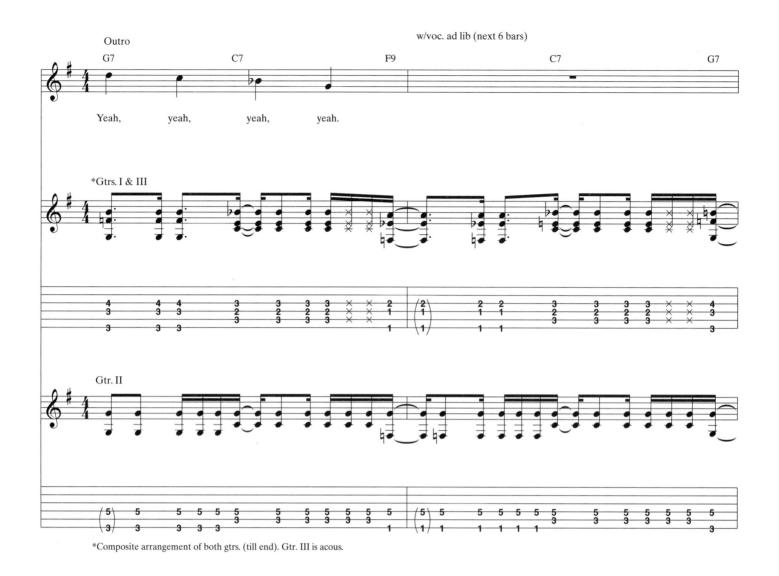

Yeah, yeah, yeah, yeah.

*Composite arrangement of both gtrs. (till end). Gtr. III is acous.

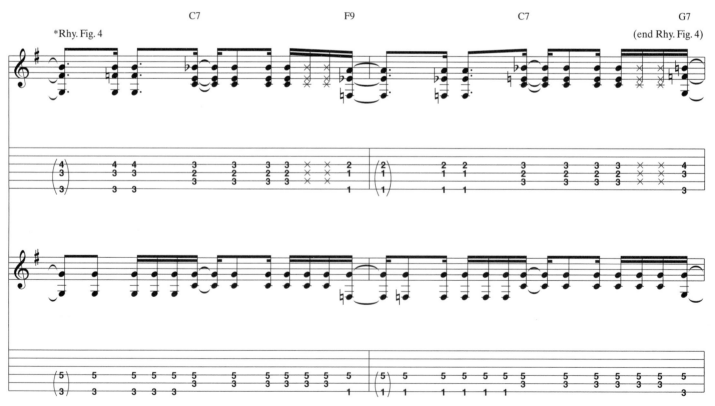

*Play w/variations ad lib when recalled.

THE LAST STOP

Words and Music by
David J. Matthews and Stefan Lessard

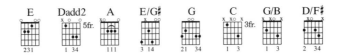

Moderate Rock ♩ = 108

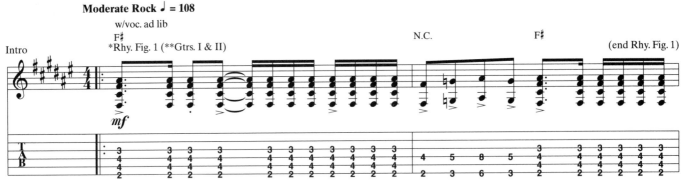

*Play all guitar parts w/slight variations ad lib when repeated or recalled (throughout).
**Acous.; composite arrangement of both gtrs. till otherwise indicated.

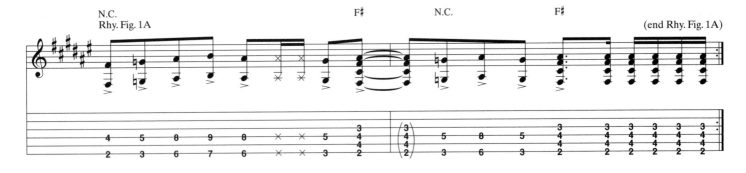

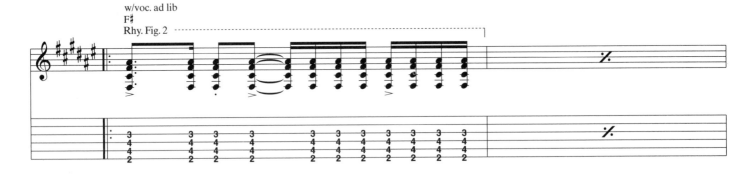

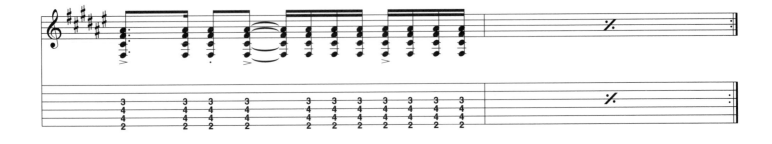

*Tune down 1/2 step (low to high): E♭ A♭ D♭ G♭ B♭ E♭. Music sounds 1/2 step lower than indicated.
Gtr. IV is two acous. gtrs. arr. for one; Gtr. V is banjo arr. for gtr. and plays w/variations ad lib on repeats.

Additional Lyrics

2. Oh, no. Gracious, even God
   Bloodied the cross. Your sins are washed enough.
   Mothers cry, "Is hate so deep?
   Must my baby's bones this hungry fire feed?"
   As smoke clouds roll in the symphony of death,
   This is the last stop.
   Oh, scream. *(To Pre-chorus)*

DON'T DRINK THE WATER

Words and Music by
David J. Matthews

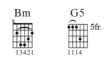

*Drop-D tuning:
⑥ = D

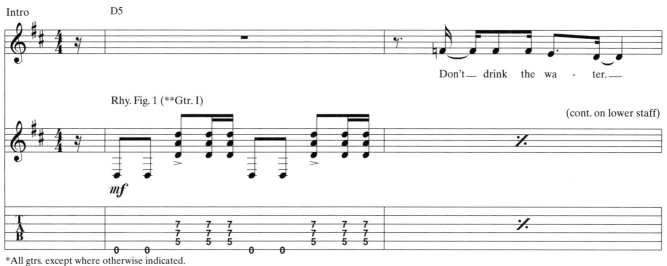

*All gtrs. except where otherwise indicated.

**Two acous. gtrs. arr. for one.

*Banjo arr. for gtr.
Open-D tuning (low to high): D A D F♯ A D

1st Verse
D5

Come out,   come out,   no___ use   in___ hid - ing.___

Riff A

*w/slide
let ring
w/o slide
w/slide
let ring
w/o slide
w/slide

Rhy. Fig. 2

*Wear slide on pinky.

w/Riff A (6 times)

(Gtr. I)

(end Rhy. Fig. 2)

*w/Rhy. Fig. 2 (3 times)

Come   now,   come   now,___   can   you   not___   see?

*Play all gtr. parts w/slight variations
ad lib when recalled (throughout).

33

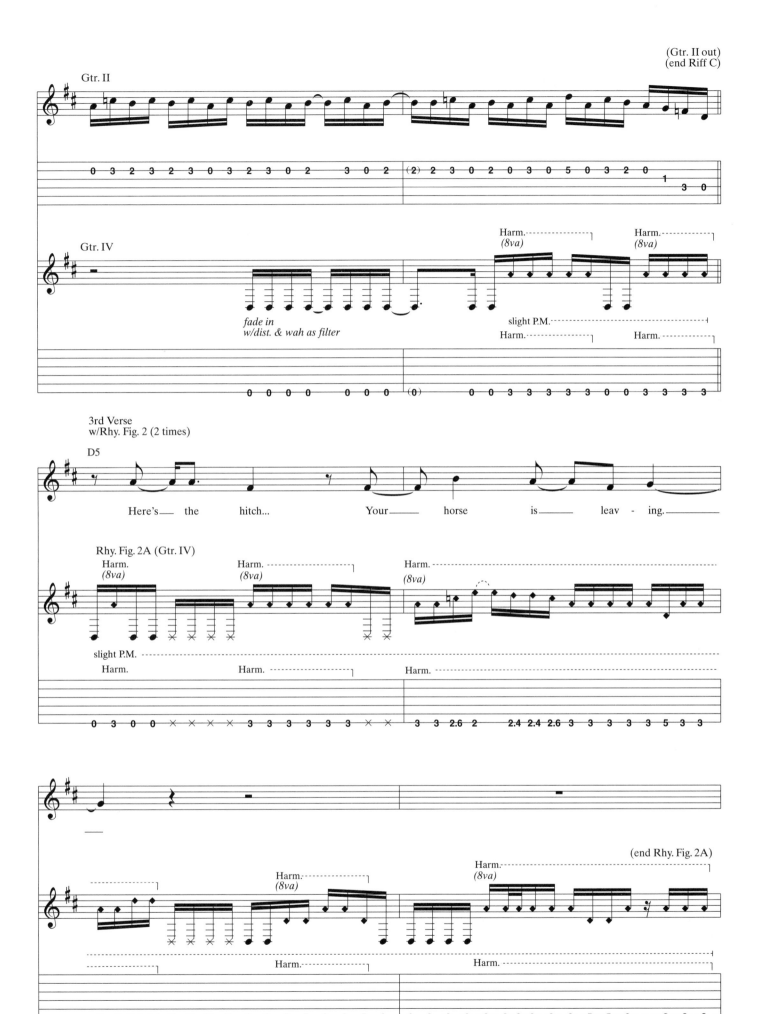

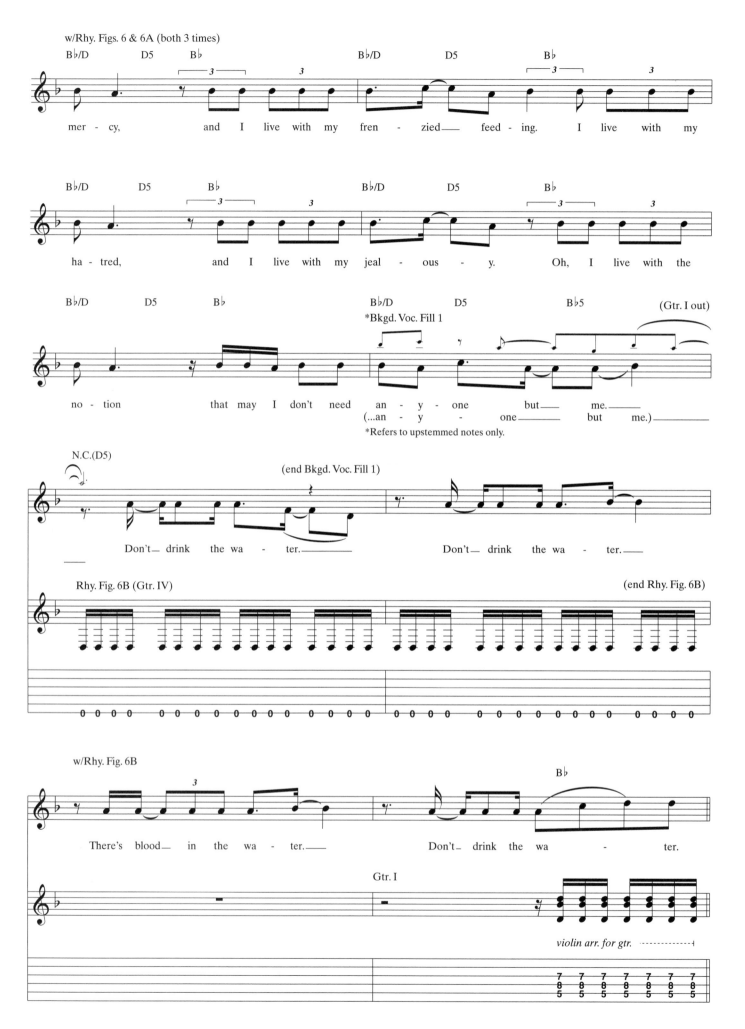

Segue to "Stay"

STAY (WASTING TIME)

Words and Music by David J. Matthews,
Stefan Lessard, and Leroi Moore

*Play all gtr. parts w/slight variations ad lib when repeated or recalled (throughout).
**Acous.

45

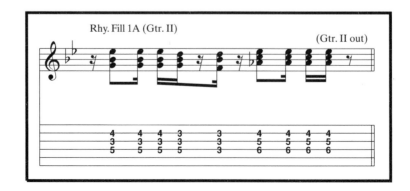

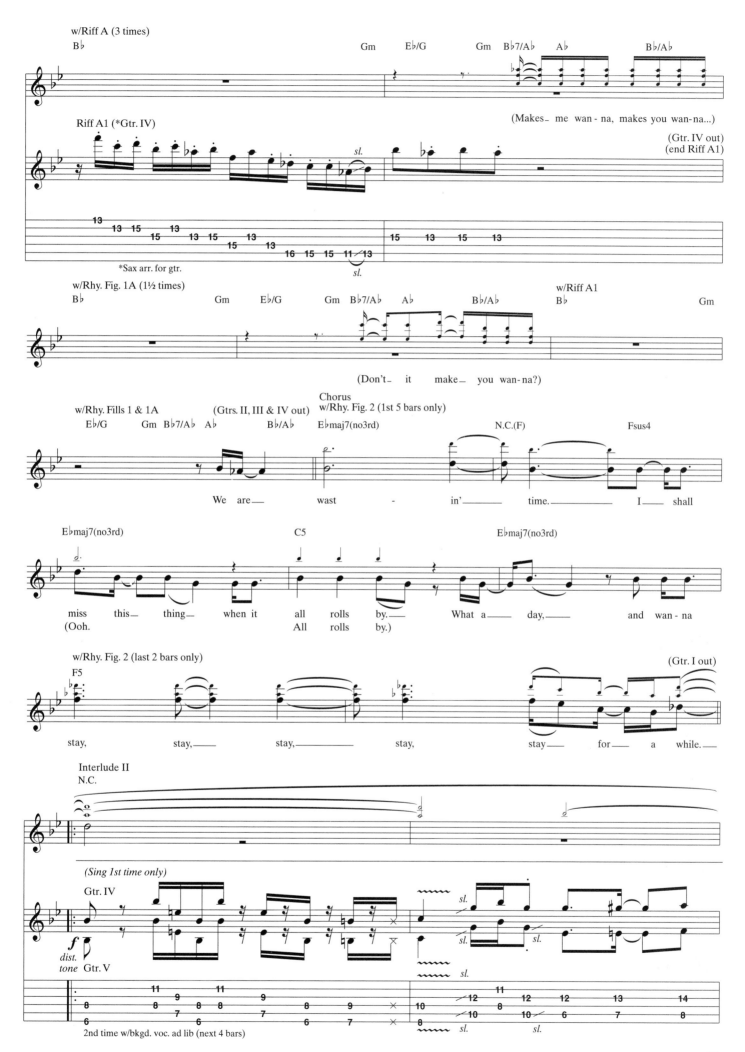

Additional Lyrics

2. Well, then later on the sun began to fade.
   And then, well, the clouds rolled over our heads,
   And it began to rain.
   Oh, we were dancin', mouths open,
   We were splashin' in the tongue taste.
   And for a moment, this good time would never end.
   You and me, you and me...

2nd Chorus:
Just wastin' time.
I was kissin' you, you were kissin' me, love,
From a good day into the moonlight.
Now a night so fine makes us wanna
Stay, stay, stay, stay, stay for a while. *(To Interlude I)*

HALLOWEEN

Words and Music by
David J. Matthews

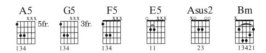

*Strings arr. for gtr. **Acous.

*The lyrics to this song have
been intentionally omitted.

1st Verse
w/Rhy. Fig. 1 (4 times)
N.C.(F)

Rhy. Fig. 1A (Gtr. II)

(end Rhy. Fig. 1A)

w/Rhy. Fig. 1A (3 times)

Chorus
A5

G5

Rhy. Fig. 2
(Gtrs. I & II)

F5

E5

(end Rhy. Fig. 2)

w/Rhy. Fig. 2
A5

G5

F5

54

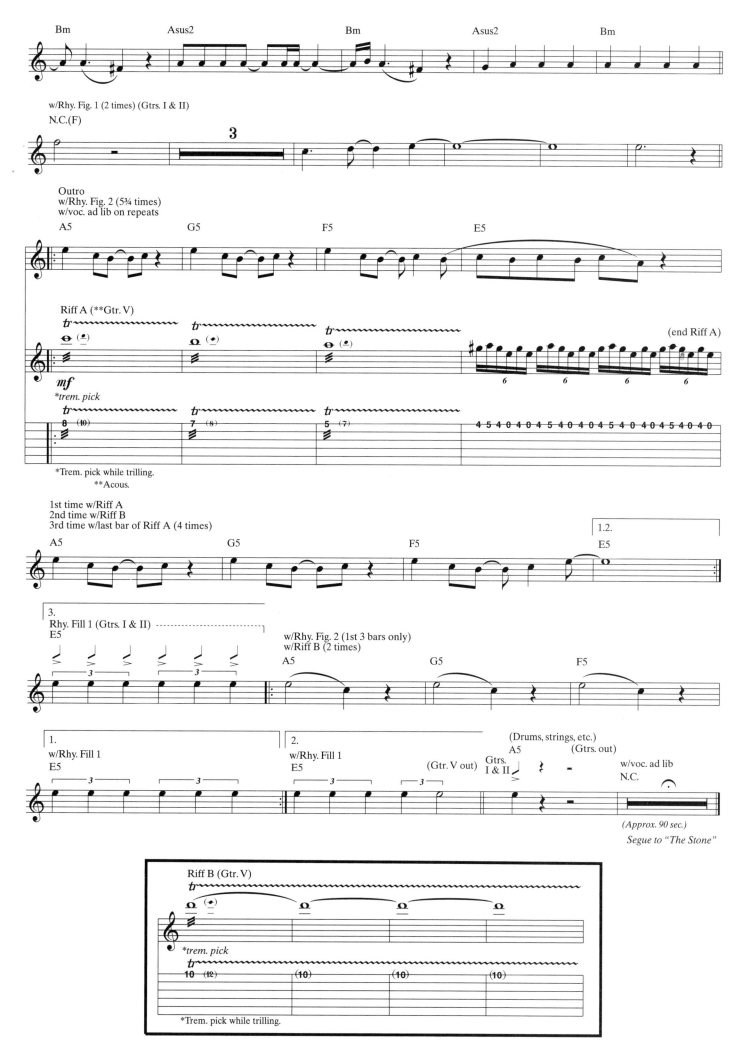

THE STONE

Words and Music by
David J. Matthews

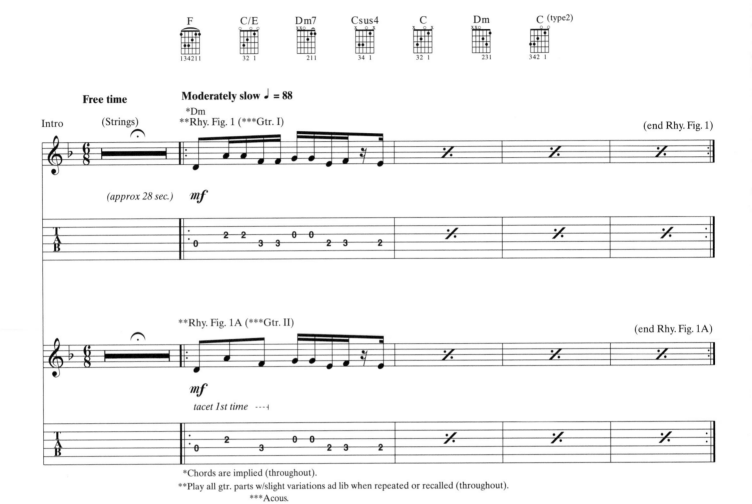

*Chords are implied (throughout).
**Play all gtr. parts w/slight variations ad lib when repeated or recalled (throughout).
***Acous.

*Violin arr. for gtr. (next 4 bars only).

57

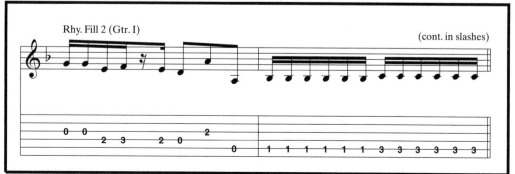

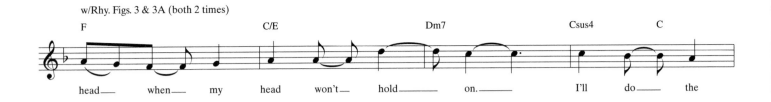

head___ when___ my head won't___ hold_____ on.___ I'll do___ the

same___ if___ the same's what___ you___ want. { 1. And / 2.3. But } if not___ I'll

go,_____ I___ will___ go a - lone._____ 3. I'm

Rhy. Fig. 4 (Gtr. I)

grad. cresc.

Rhy. Fig. 4A (Gtr. II)

grad. cresc.

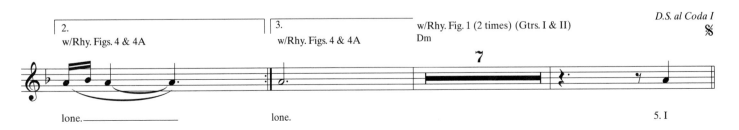

2.
w/Rhy. Figs. 4 & 4A

3.
w/Rhy. Figs. 4 & 4A

w/Rhy. Fig. 1 (2 times) (Gtrs. I & II)
Dm

D.S. al Coda I

lone._____ lone. 5. I

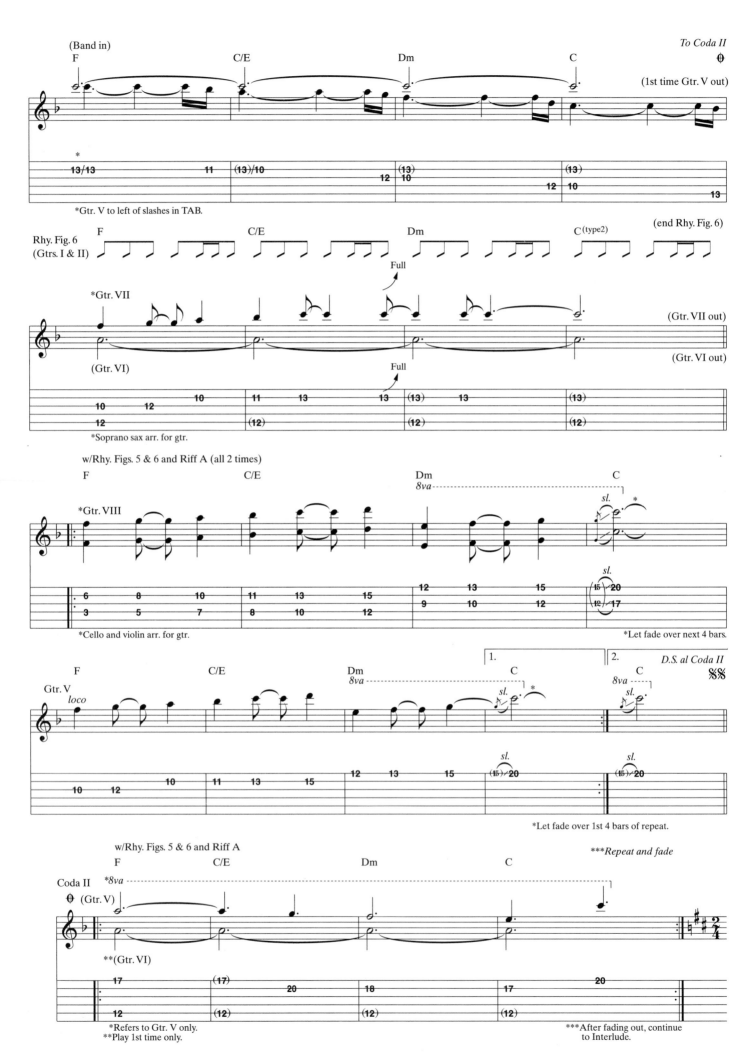

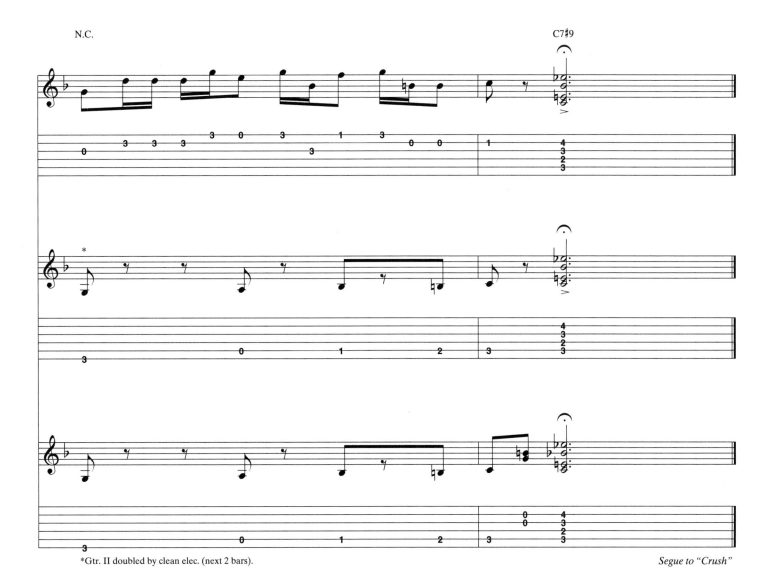

*Gtr. II doubled by clean elec. (next 2 bars).

Segue to "Crush"

Additional Lyrics

3. I'm a long way,
   Oh, from that fool's mistake.
   And now forever pay.
   No, run, I will run and I'll be okay.
   I was just... *(To Chorus)*

4. A long way
   To bury the past, for I don't want to pay.
   Oh, how I wish this:
   To turn back the clock and do over again.
   Now I'm just... *(To Chorus)*

5. I need so
   To say in your arms, see you smile, hold you close.
   And now it weighs on me
   As heavy as stone and a bone-chilling cold.
   I was just... *(To Outro)*

CRUSH

Words and Music by
David J. Matthews

*Composite arrangement of both gtrs. unless otherwise indicated (throughout).

**Acous. w/drop-D tuning

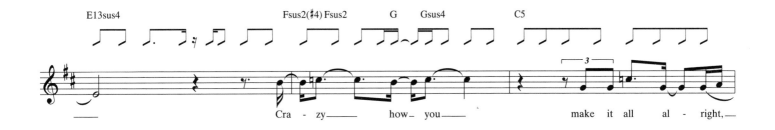

Cra - zy____ how_ you____ make it all al - right,____

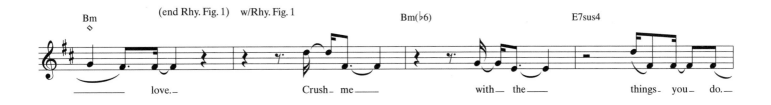

____ love.__ Crush_ me____ with_ the____ things_ you do.__

And I____ do____ for_ you____ an - y - thing_ too,____

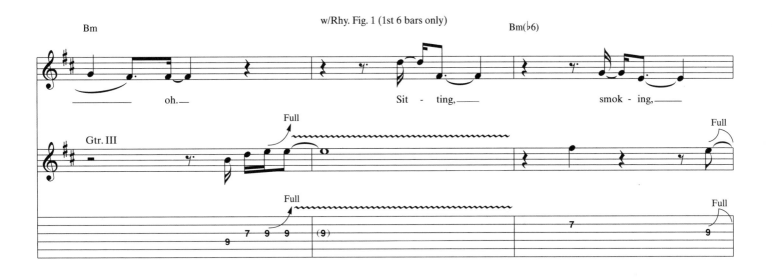

____ oh.__ Sit - ting,____ smok - ing,____

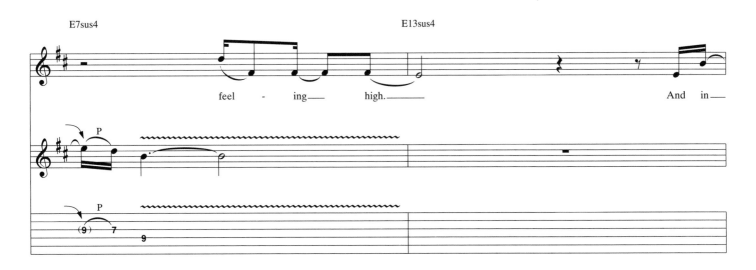

feel - ing____ high.____ And in____

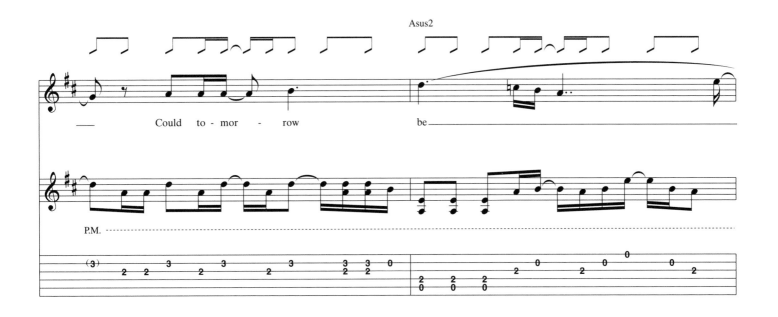

Could to-mor-row be

(end Rhy. Fig. 2)

so won-drous as you there, sleep - ing?

2nd Verse
w/Rhy. Fig. 1

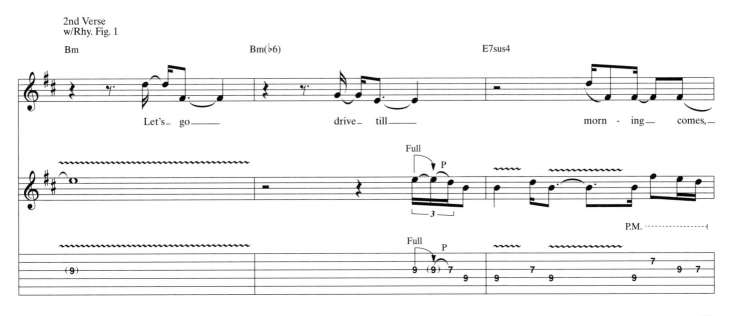

Let's go drive till morn-ing comes,

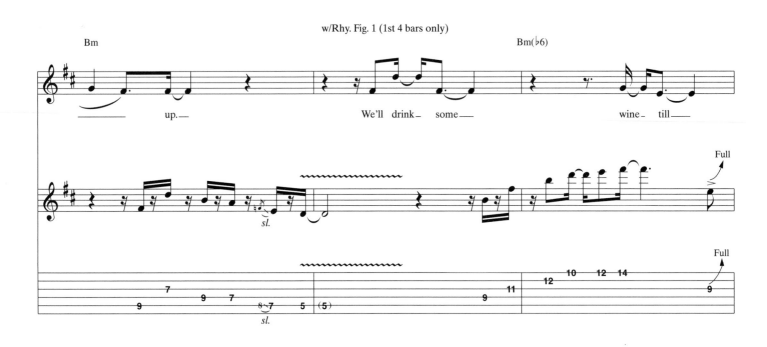

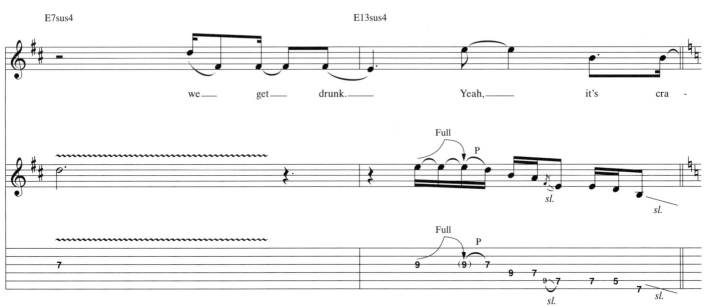

70

*Play w/slight variations ad lib when recalled (throughout).

Pre-chorus
w/Rhy. Figs. 2 & *2A

Love - ly la - dy,_____   I will treat_ you   sweet - ly,___

*w/slight variations ad lib

_____ a - dore_ you.____ I___ mean you crush_ me.___ And it's times like_ these_

_____ when my faith_ I   feel,_____ and_____ I___ know

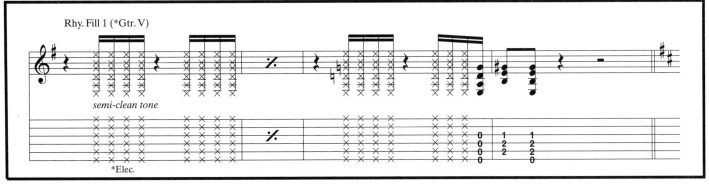

Rhy. Fill 1 (*Gtr. V)

semi-clean tone

*Elec.

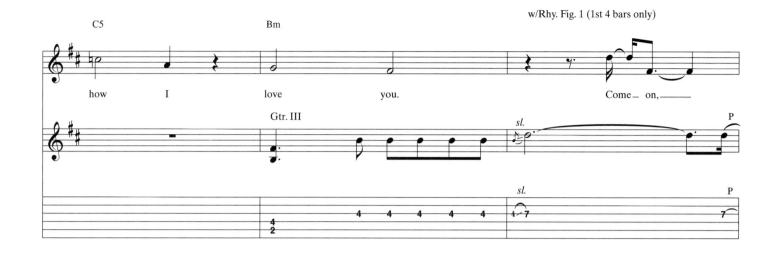

how I love you. Come on,

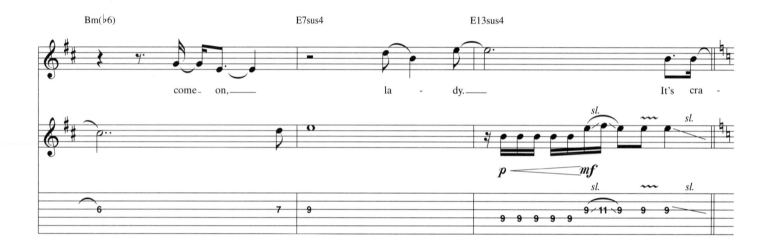

come on, la-dy. It's cra-

Chorus
w/Rhy. Figs. 3, 3A & 3B (all 1st 4 bars only)

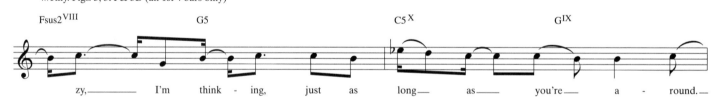

zy, I'm think-ing, just as long as you're a-round.

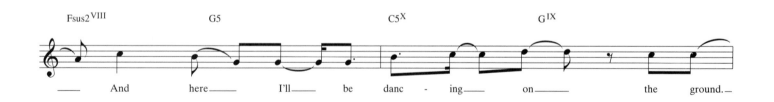

And here I'll be danc-ing on the ground.

w/Rhy. Figs. 3, 3A & 3B (all bars 3 & 4 only) (all 5½ times)

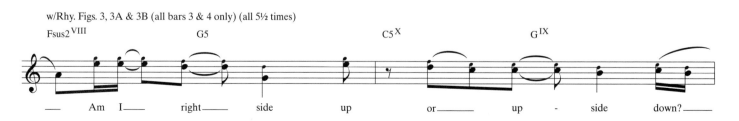

Am I right side up or up-side down?

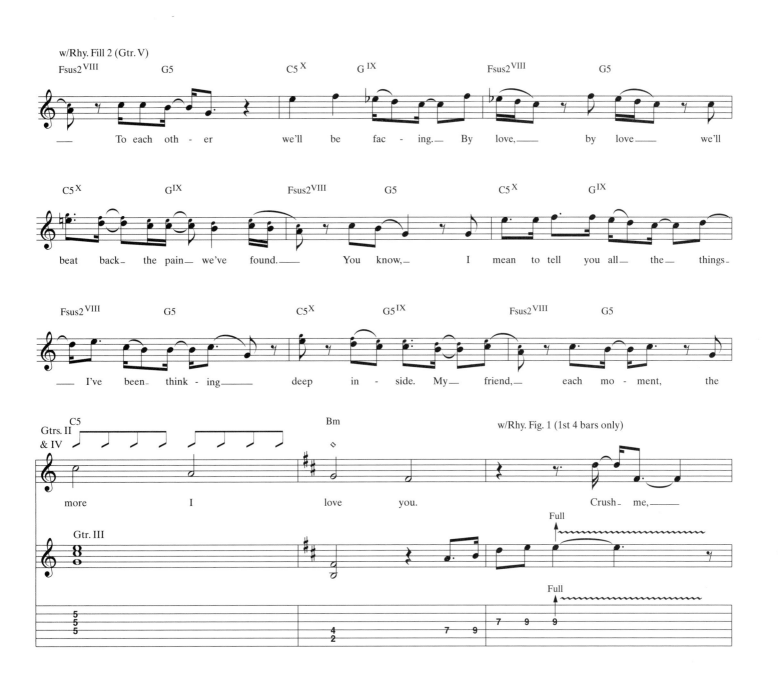

To each oth - er we'll be fac - ing. By love, by love we'll

beat back the pain we've found. You know, I mean to tell you all the things

I've been think - ing deep in - side. My friend, each mo - ment, the

more I love you. Crush me,

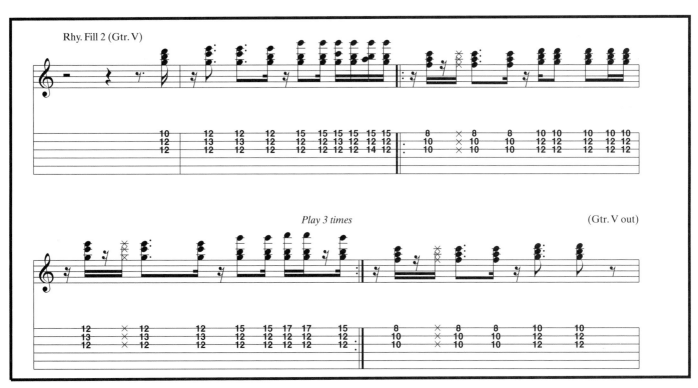

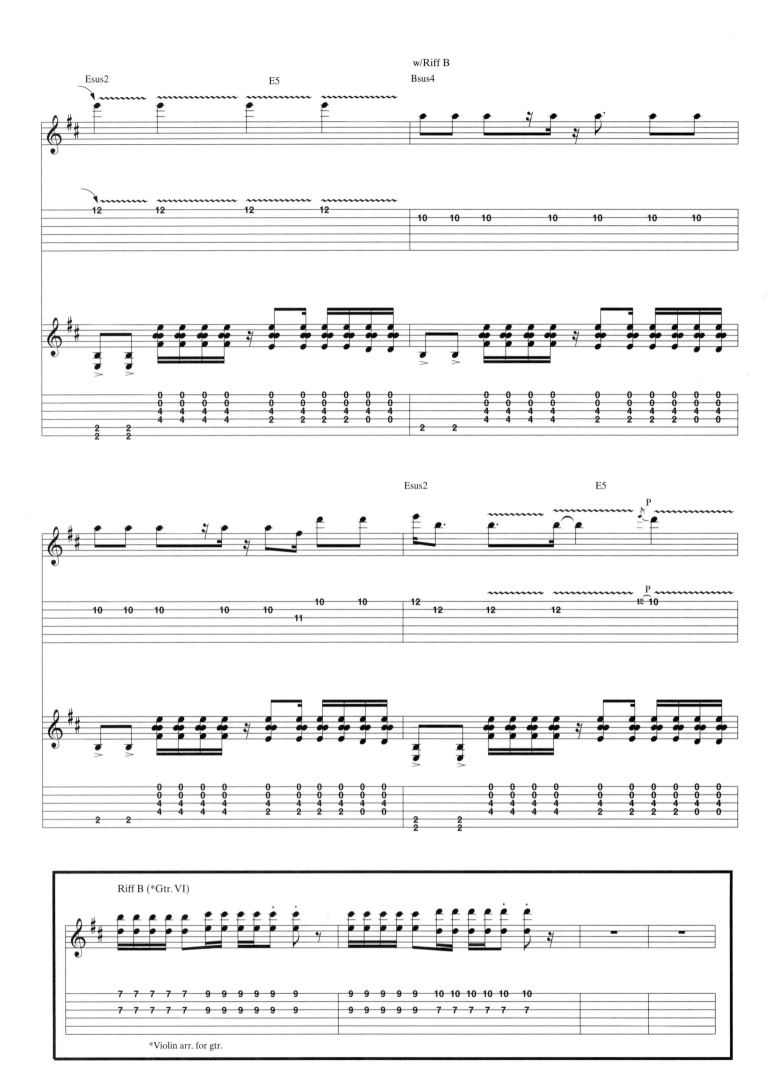

THE DREAMING TREE

Words and Music by
David J. Matthews and Stefan Lessard

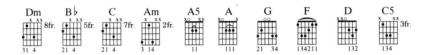

*Chord names in parentheses are implied by bass beginning 3rd time; 1st 2 times N.C.
**Acous.

*Acous. (both gtrs.)
**Bass plays D pedal when Rhy. Fig. 2 is played (throughout).

died.   The air— is grow-ing thick,   a fear— he can-not hide.   The dream-ing tree has

Interlude
w/Rhy. Fig. 3 (8 times)

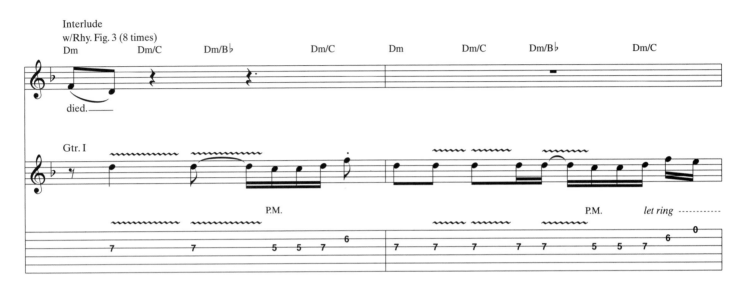

died.—

Gtr. I

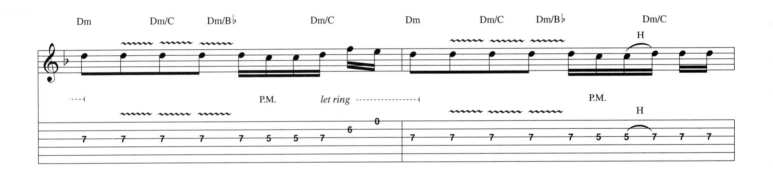

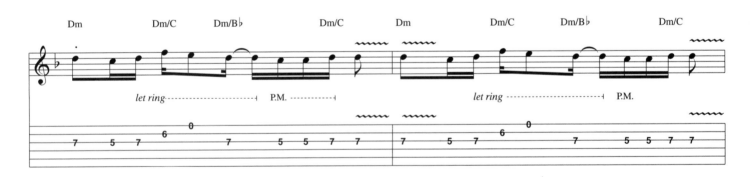

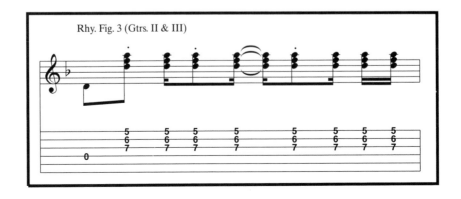

Rhy. Fig. 3 (Gtrs. II & III)

*With one of gtr.'s vol. knobs set to zero, flick toggle switch to "on" position in rhythm indicated (next 7 bars).

91

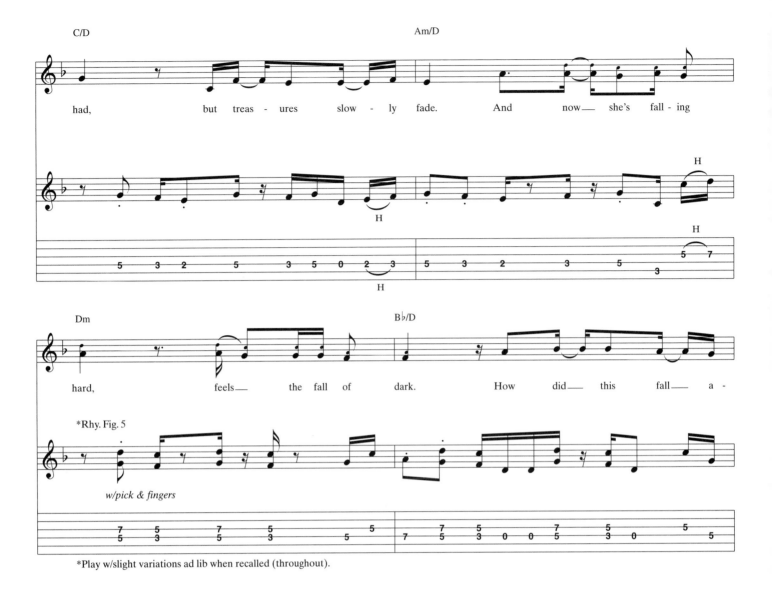

*Play w/slight variations ad lib when recalled (throughout).

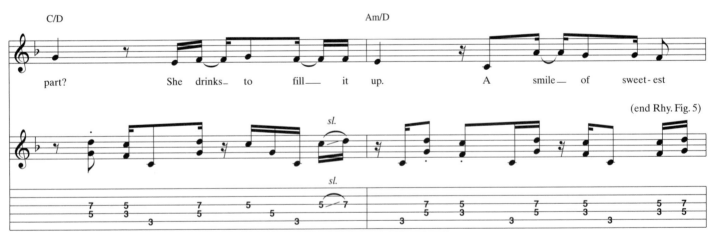

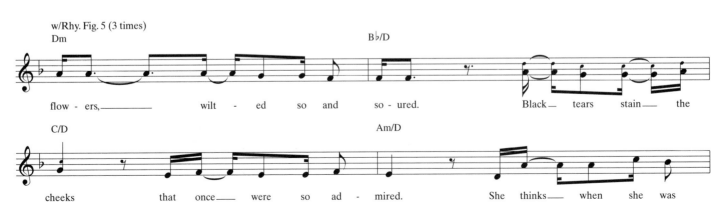

talk? Can— you take— pit - y?——— I— don't ask—

much, but won't you speak, please?———

w/Rhy. Fig. 1 (2½ times)

*N.C.(A5)

Gtr. III

*Chords implied by bass (next 10 bars only).

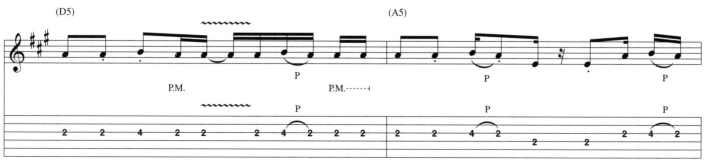

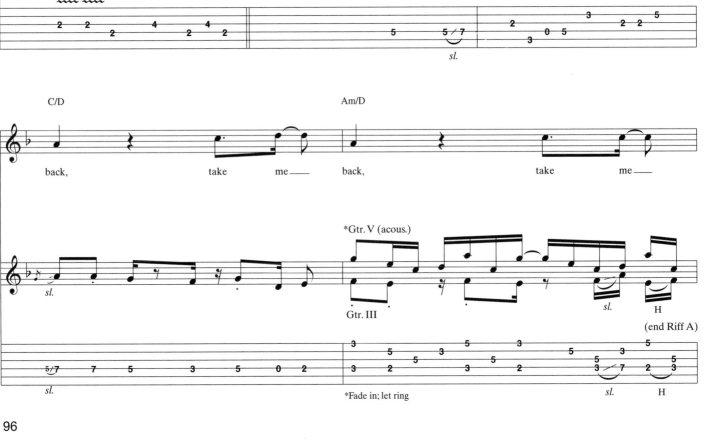

PIG

Words and Music by
David J. Matthews, Stefan Lessard,
Carter Beauford, Leroi Moore, and Boyd Tinsley

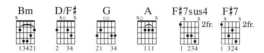

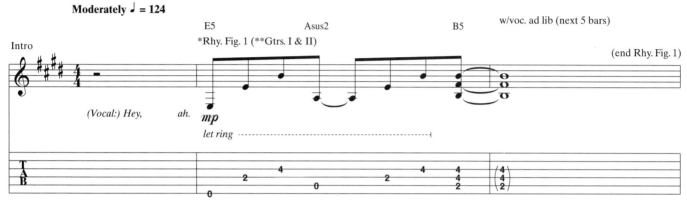

*Play all gtr. parts w/slight variations ad lib when recalled (throughout).

**Acous. (both gtrs.)

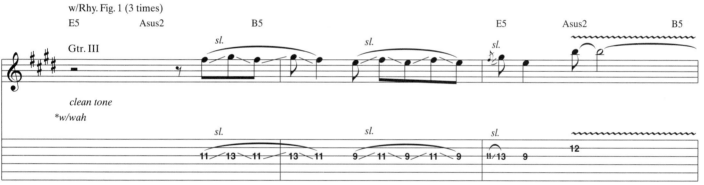

*Rock pedal back and forth ad lib (throughout).

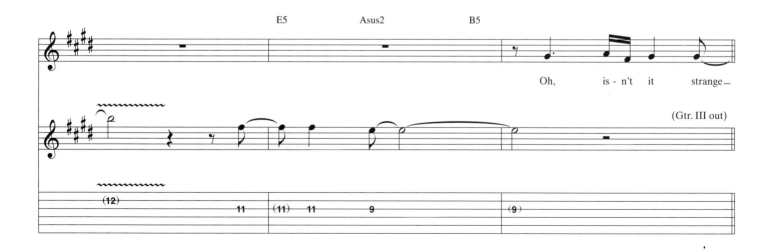

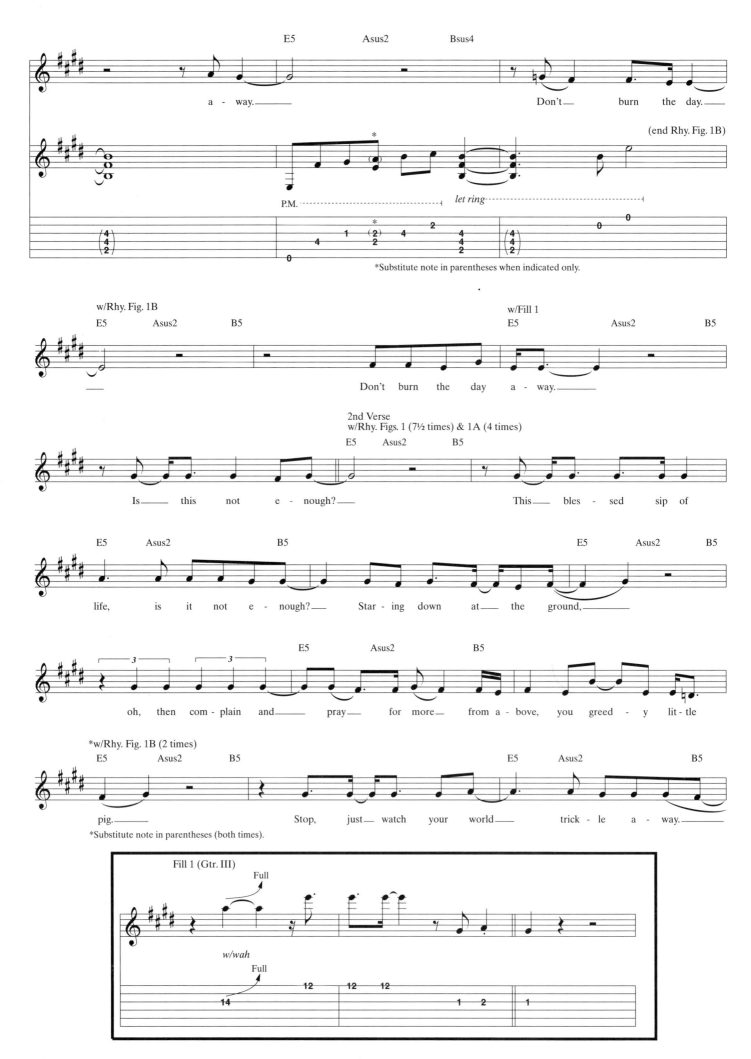

*Substitute note in parentheses when indicated only.

*Substitute note in parentheses (both times).

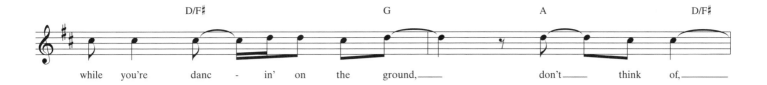

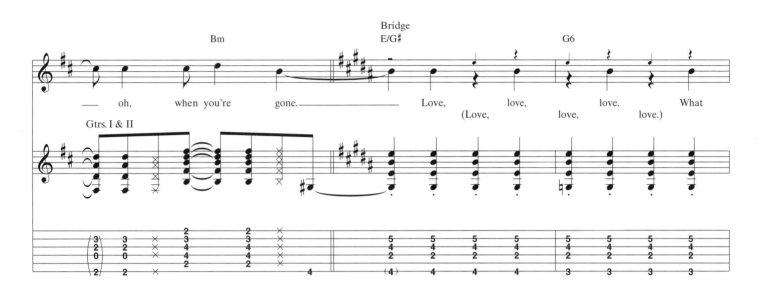

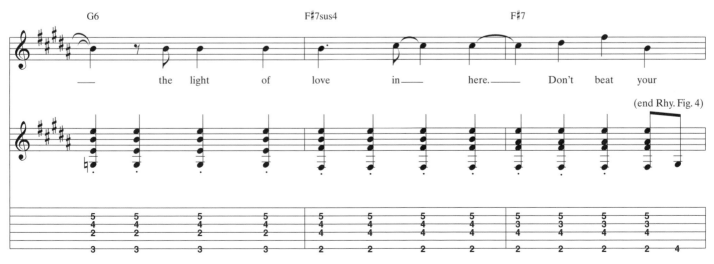

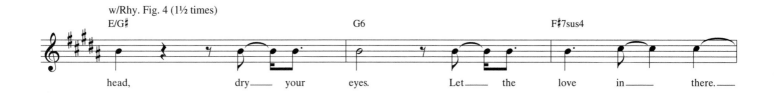

w/Rhy. Fig. 4 (1½ times)

head, dry your eyes. Let the love in there.

To Coda ⊕

There's bad times, {but / well,} that's o - kay. Just look for

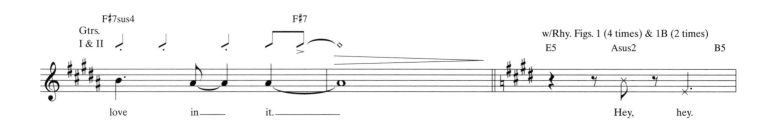

love in it. Hey, hey.

And don't burn the day a - way.

3rd Verse
w/Rhy. Figs. 1 (4 times) & 1B (2 times)

Look, here are we_____ on this star-ry_____ night

(Gtr. III out)

_____ star-in' in-to space._____ And I_____ must say_____

I feel as small as dust ly-in' down_____ here, oh._____

Pre - chorus
*w/Rhy. Fig. 2 (7½ times)

What point could there be trou-b'ling? Head down,_____ won-d'ring what_____

*w/strumming variations ad lib

_____ will be-come of me. Why con-cern,_____ we can-not see,_____ mm,-

_____ but no rea-son to a-ban-don it._____ But time_____ is short, time,

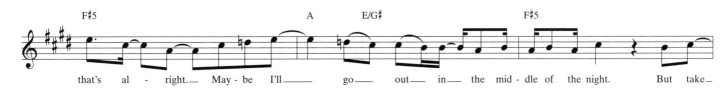

that's al - right. May-be I'll_____ go_____ out_____ in_____ the mid-dle of the night. But take-

_____ your hands_____ now from your eyes,_____ my love. All_____ good things must come_____ to an end_____

w/Rhy. Fill 2

w/Rhy. Figs. 1 (3 times) & 1B (1½ times)

_____ some time._____ Oh, but don't burn the day_____

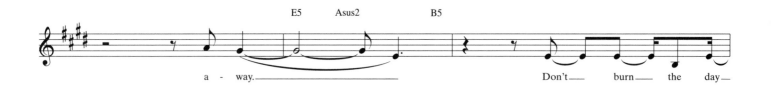

a - way._____ Don't _____ burn_____ the day_____

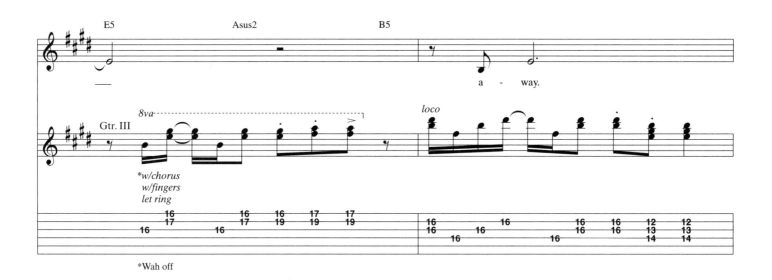

a - way.

Gtr. III

*w/chorus
w/fingers
let ring

*Wah off

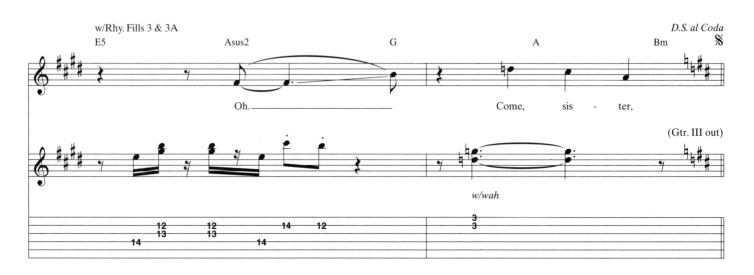

w/Rhy. Fills 3 & 3A

D.S. al Coda

Oh._____ Come, sis - ter,

(Gtr. III out)

w/wah

love   in_____   it.   Yeah._____

_____   Just   let   the   love   in_____   there._____   Oh,   love..._____

*After fading out, continue to Interlude.

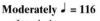

Moderately ♩ = 116

Interlude
w/voc. ad lib (till end)
N.C.
Gtrs. I & II

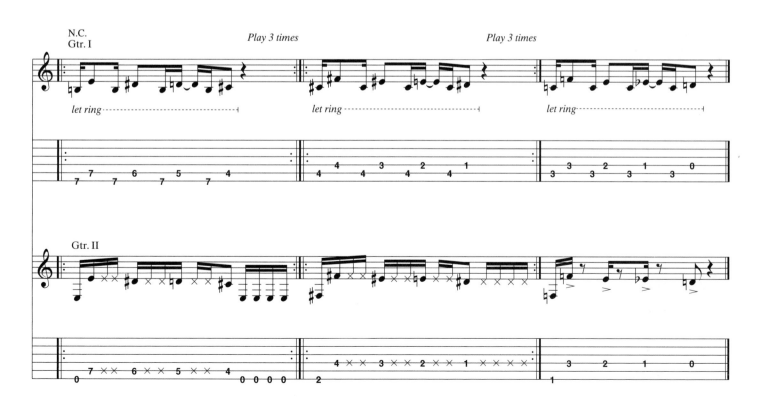

SPOON

Words and Music by
David J. Matthews

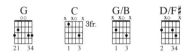

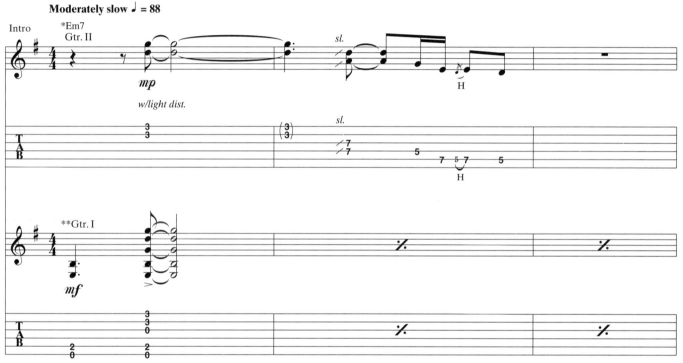

*Some chords are implied (throughout).
**Two acous. gtrs. arr. for one (throughout).

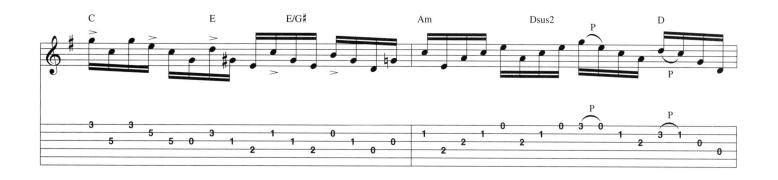

Laugh - ing out _____ loud. _____

4th Verse
w/Rhy. Fig. 1 (2 times)

4. From time to ___ time, ___

(Gtr. III out)

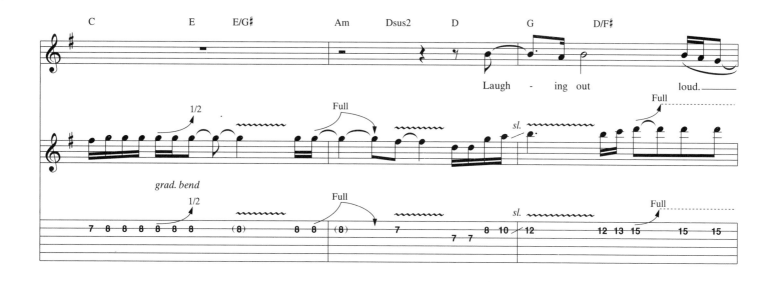

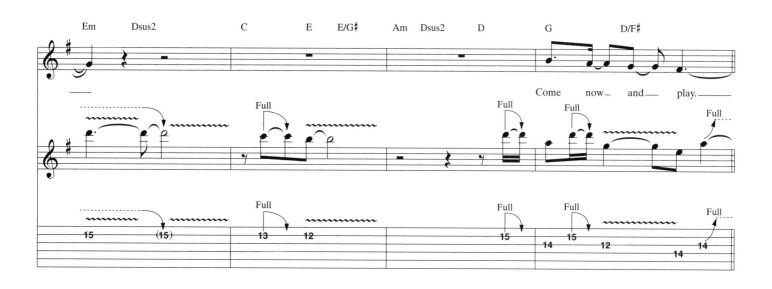

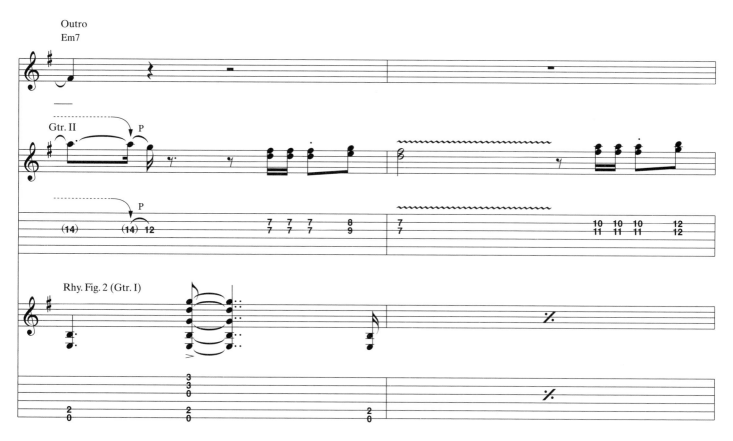

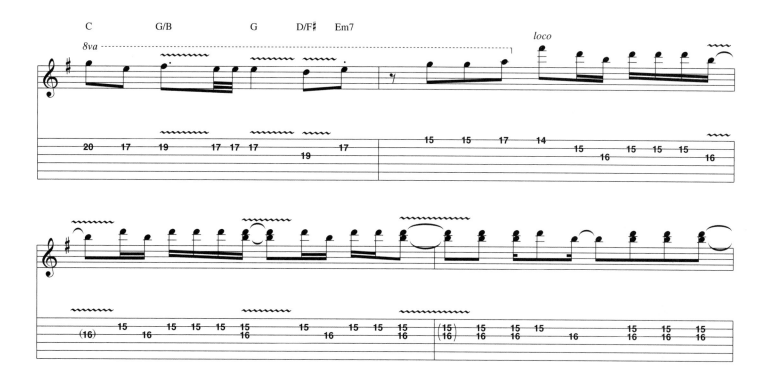

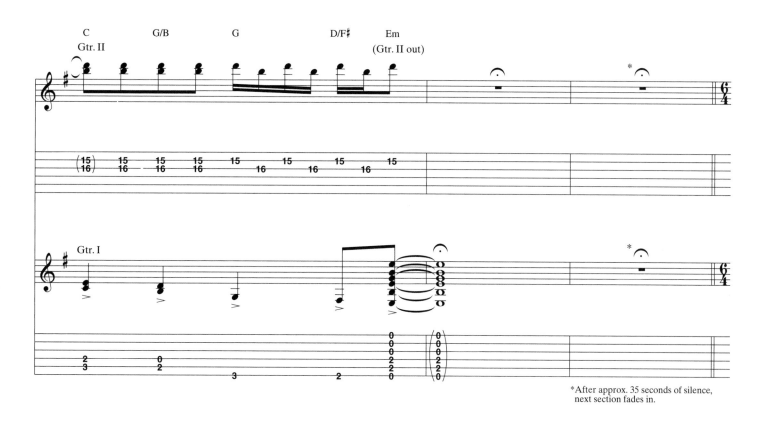

*After approx. 35 seconds of silence, next section fades in.

*Tune down ½ step (low to high:) Eb Ab Db Gb Bb Eb. All music sounds ½ step lower than indicated (till end). Gtr. IV is two acous. gtrs. arr. for one.

w/Rhy. Fig. 3 (7 times)

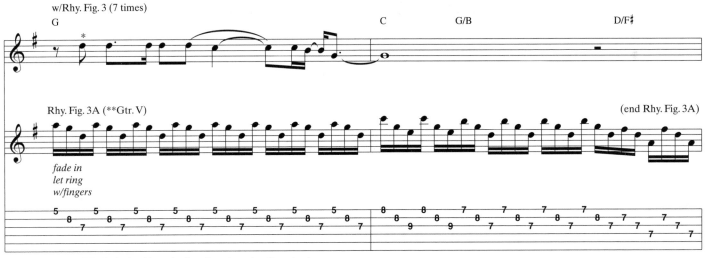

Rhy. Fig. 3A (**Gtr. V)   (end Rhy. Fig. 3A)

fade in
let ring
w/fingers

*The lyrics for this section have been intentionally omitted.
**Tune down ½ step as before. Gtr. V is banjo arr. for gtr. and plays Rhy. Fig. 3A w/variations ad lib when recalled (till end).

w/Rhy. Fig. 3A (6 times)

w/Rhy. Figs. 3 & 3A   *Repeat and fade*

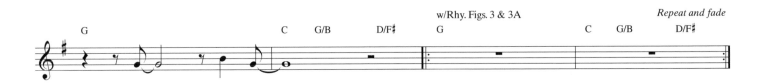

Additional Lyrics

3. Spoon in, spoon stirring my coffee.
I thought of this and turned to the gate.
But on my way, crack, lightning and then thunder.
I hid my head and the storm slipped away. Well... *(To Chorus)*